BRITAIN
IN OLD PHOTOGRAPHS

PINNER & HATCH END

Past & Present

Don Walter

Sutton Publishing Limited
Phoenix Mill · Thrupp · Stroud
Gloucestershire · GL5 2BU

First published 2002

Title page photograph: To celebrate the Coronation of King George V in 1911, Pinner village staged a lavish horse-drawn carnival. Here, led by the village fire brigade, the procession lines up outside Gurney's, the provision merchants.
Endpapers, front: Marsh Road had largely developed as a shopping street by 1950, although a few cottages still remain on the right-hand side. *Back*: With a substantial office block replacing the last few remaining homes, Marsh Road currently presents a picture of commercial activity of a kind seen throughout London's boroughs.

British Library Cataloguing in Publication Data
A catalogue record for this book is available from the British Library.

ISBN 0-7509-2987-1

Typeset in 10.5/13.5 Photina.
Typesetting and origination by
Sutton Publishing Limited.
Printed and bound in England by
J.H. Haynes & Co. Ltd, Sparkford.

Fields adjoining the railway near Cannon Lane go under the plough as part of a First World War agricultural drive. This view was taken in about 1915 from the Cannon Lane bridge on the railway's Rayners Lane–Eastcote stretch.

CONTENTS

Even if the quick glance suggests that shopping in and around the High Street is much as it always has been, closer study reveals a somewhat different story. Most of the family-run businesses, such as Harry Lines's ironmongery shop (then at no. 34) in 1900, have now disappeared. Instead we find boutiques, restaurants, estate agents, even major supermarkets – the latter put up with some skill and not a little controversy.

INTRODUCTION

The first thing to be said about Pinner's past and present is that the gulf between the two is nowhere near as wide or as visible as the changes that have racked – or, as some would say, wrecked – other communities equally close to our capital city. Pinner High Street is still recognisably the picturesque village street which, for well over a hundred years, has captured the imagination of countless photographers. Indeed, in the London Borough of Harrow, only Harrow on the Hill (featured in an earlier volume in this series) can point to a comparable record of conservation.

This is not so much a matter of Pinner's good fortune as of the good judgement shown by its residents and, especially, the good stewardship maintained by such bodies as the local authority and the Pinner Association, formed well before the Second World War and now some 4,000 members strong.

For all its strengths, the Pinner Association recently proved powerless against the Parliamentary Boundary Commission which has proposed separating Pinner and Hatch End from the Harrow West constituency in order to create a new constituency to be called Ruislip, Northwood and Pinner. To anyone with the slightest sense of history, this is an incongruous decision, for Pinner and Harrow have always been close in far more than a geographical sense.

In early days, Pinner was an integral part not only of the Manor of Harrow (as recorded in the Domesday Book) but also of the Parish of St Mary's, Harrow on the Hill. Moreover, three of the four estates – Pinner Park, Woodhall and Headstone – belonging to the Lord of the Manor were actually the boundaries of present-day Pinner.

Following the precedent set by Harrow, whose annual fair and weekly market received royal assent as early as 1261, Pinner had its own fair from about 1336. Now probably the event for which Pinner is best known, the fair originally marked the birthday of St John the Baptist, to whom the medieval village church is dedicated, but in more recent times it has moved to the Wednesday after the Spring Bank Holiday.

In common with its Middlesex neighbours, Pinner remained a largely agricultural community for centuries with only a few great houses scattered among its many farms. Surprisingly perhaps, not all of these farms have totally disappeared. Grazing cows can still be glimpsed from the dual carriageway of King George V Avenue which, for decades, has cut Pinner Park Farm in two; as recently as May 2002 the local press reported that some thirty of its farm animals had fallen victim to marauding foxes.

Pinnerwood Farm currently maintains a successful commercial stud while several of the buildings of Pinner Hill Farm have been handsomely restored – although admittedly for non-agricultural pursuits. Some, like John Claudius Loudon's Woodhall Farm, have become private homes or, like Hatch End Farm, business premises. Many more, however, are remembered only by the evocative naming of the residential roads that have replaced them.

A few of the grand houses also remain. The early eighteenth-century Pinner House still stands in Church Lane but with the addition of a modern wing offering sheltered accommodation to the elderly. A small part of West House, where Nelson's grandson made his home in the 1870s, can still be seen at the heart of Pinner's War Memorial Park. What's more, the success of a current Pinner Association appeal may yet see its transformation into a museum devoted to the work of another of the district's former residents, the humourist William Heath Robinson. For the rest, Pinner's homes are strictly, though nicely, suburban.

Their spread can be directly linked to the coming of the railway. Harrow and Wealdstone station opened in 1837 on the first London–Birmingham line, and it was not long before the good people of Pinner pressed persistently for a station of their own. This was duly opened in 1842 and called Pinner even though it was sited at Hatch End about a mile and a half from the village itself. Then, within a decade, the Woodridings Estate had been built near the line and the present-day Hatch End station was born.

So what are the we to make of Pinner and Hatch End in 2002? For a start it is now considered a very desirable place to live. This is especially true of people with money, a fact reflected in the amazing number of up-market shops and restaurants that line the commercial streets. Nevertheless a closer examination of the whole area reveals a more diverse social mix than might at first be apparent with properties that exemplify the twin meanings of 'estate' within what the cynical might call 'mugging distance' of each other.

Nor is the area immune from many of the blights of twenty-first century living. For example, the closure of the public toilets in Chapel Lane was recently demanded by the local drug squad at much the same time as fellow police officers trapped cocaine dealers operating at Pinner station. Grafitti is all too frequently found, as I discovered when taking the modern photographs in this volume – empty shops (of which more and more seem likely to appear) being among the more obvious targets. Yet, in general, the village (as locals still proudly regard it) has managed to find a reasonably harmonious balance between the forces of progress and the demands of preservation. Nevertheless, this has not been achieved without controversy.

As long ago as 1966, a proposal to build a seven-storey block of flats and a precinct of some fifteen shops behind the High Street caused a ripple of shock. Though the project never got off the ground, residents remained on their guard and a subsequent proposal to cut through the High Street to build the district's first food hall (on much the same site) was viewed with considerable anxiety.

In the event, and thanks in part to early negotiations with the Pinner Association, the project was completed to general satisfaction. However, a precedent had been set, and within a few years, Sainsburys applied to cut a passage through the other side of the High Street giving access to a new superstore on what had once been the car park for Pinner Metropolitan station. This time, however, most people felt that the proposed scale was wholly alien to the village, the selling space for the new store being some fifteen times greater than that of the previous Sainsburys store in Bridge Street.

Hundreds packed a meeting to protest against what one Pinner notable described as 'the worst act of vandalism since the Vikings'. In this instance, the interests of big business ultimately prevailed, although it is probably true to say that the resulting superstore is now patronised by former protesters as much as anyone else. However, there can be no doubt that the immediate environs of Pinner station are currently more evocative of a new town than an old village.

The construction of two new supermarkets inevitably created two new addresses – Barters Walk and Bishops Walk. Of the two, the latter sounds especially appropriate with its suggestion of those far-off days when the archbishops of Canterbury, lords of the manor of Harrow (and Pinner) held court at nearby Headstone. But, truth to tell, the roadway was actually named after Bishops Stores, the first retailers on the site!

While no one can pretend that this is an especially important fact in the overall history of Pinner, it does underline a significant truth – and conveniently brings us back to the starting point of this introduction. In the year 2002 it is increasingly difficult to assess where Pinner's past ends – and its present and future begin.

Don Walter, November 2002

1

High Street

The old High Street remains the great glory of present-day Pinner. Indeed, it was already
centuries old when this engraving was made in about 1828, recording such landmarks as the
Queen's Head (left) and St John's parish church that have changed remarkably little with the
passage of time. Unusually, many current High Street buildings are even older than they
appear, since later additions now cover sixteenth-century timber framing.

From the very earliest days of photography the picturesque charms of the High Street have attracted photographers, resulting in an invaluable record of its nineteenth-century past. Here a mother and pram and a horse and cart, share the same roadway without the benefit of a pavement in about 1872.

By the mid-1880s the High Street had pavements on both sides, a necessity, given the rough nature of the road itself, particularly at its lower end near the flood-prone River Pinn. The Crown Inn (left), once the terminus for a London-bound coach, closed in 1896.

By 1908 the High Street looked more like the busy shopping street it has become. On the right photographer Mary Emery (who may have taken this picture) had opened a Photographic Bazaar in a block of four tall buildings put up by Pinner resident Daniel Gurney. Locals initially called it 'The Barracks' either because of its bleak architecture or because it housed an early headquarters of the Salvation Army.

In the early twentieth century Sid Hedges of East End Farm would often drive his cattle through the heart of the village. Nevertheless it is said that an unknown photographer was so pleased to capture this scene for posterity that he willingly paid Hedges £1 for the privilege!

This souvenir of King George V's Coronation gives us another glimpse of the Queen's Head public house, the history of which is charted over the next few pages. Despite the prominent '1705' on the façade, it is now accepted that one Margery Bateman kept a tavern on this site as early as 1636.

Opposite: In 1912 the licensee of the Queen's Head added a live bear to its list of attractions. Although the animal spent most of its time in the stables at the rear, it was occasionally taken for a walk on a lead! Here it balances on the horsetrough that, in one form or another, has been a feature of the pub for about 120 years.

The Queen's Head, Pinner's oldest pub, in 1885. Some thirteen years earlier, Eleanor Ward, the grand-daughter of Lord Nelson and Lady Hamilton, was knocked down and killed outside its doors by a runaway horse.

Though the pub's seventeenth-century origins have never been in doubt, its early twentieth-century proprietors felt its popularity would be enhanced by a little discreet 'ageing'. In consequence, they added the Tudor-style vertical timbers that remain in place to this day.

By 1942 the Queen's Head had lost its horsetrough but gained a sturdy brick-built air-raid shelter. Its necessity was later confirmed by a Pinner Association record revealing that the air-raid siren had sounded over wartime Pinner on a staggering 1,200 occasions. After the war a replacement horsetough was installed.

Another casualty of the Second World War was the semi-circular sign reading '13 miles to London' which was felt to be of potential value to enemy parachutists! As the eagle-eyed will have spotted, the inn's sign has also changed over the years – not just in its design, but even the queens are different!

Though the pub's sign in the 1930s photograph above clearly features Elizabeth I, the year 2002 sees Queen Anne restored to favour. Ironically, evidence exists that the original queen to be so honoured was Philippa, wife of Edward III, who granted the charter establishing Pinner's annual fair in 1336.

The High Street took on an unaccustomed Continental look when Pinner celebrated Queen Elizabeth II's Golden Jubilee in June 2002. The closure of the street for the day meant that many of its restaurateurs could serve their customers not only on the pavement but also in the road itself!

The latest in a long line of troughs outside the Queen's Head served as an impromptu seat for some of the crowds who chose to celebrate the Golden Jubilee in the High Street. Hundreds more gathered at the top of the street for an outdoor multi-denominational service.

No. 4 High Street in one of its earlier roles as a boot repairing depot, *c.* 1905. Its across-the-yard neighbour was Tripps Forge. The scaffolding at the right was erected in readiness for the construction of a branch of Barclays Bank on the corner with Marsh Road.

By the 1930s, 4 High Street had become a successful barber's shop, the windows of which feature such popular hair products of the day as Vaseline Hair Tonic. At this time the original Victory public house was located around the corner in Marsh Road.

Very little about the Victory, now occupying 4 High Street, is exactly as it appears. The building is even older than the 1580 displayed on its façade, but it has only been a pub since 1958. Nor was its name likely to have been inspired by Nelson's flagship that is shown on its sign.

The current owners were recently obliged to reinstate the old Victory sign after removing it in favour of a more contemporary logo. They were possibly unaware of the name's significance; early in the twentieth century the original pub's builder had won a famous victory in a court case in which he was accused of infringing on a public right of way.

During the early years of the twentieth century, the Central Stores of F. Gurney & Son at 38–40 High Street sold groceries and provisions in the main shop and wines, beer and spirits from the adjoining premises. Here Frank Gurney stands on the steps (left) flanked by members of his substantial staff.

Past and present currently combine on the former Gurney's premises, now housing a public house and pizzeria trading as the Hand in Hand, a name that recalls the mid-nineteenth-century inn originally located on the site of the present Grange Court. Note the arched double doors where Gurney's wagons once passed into the yard behind.

Grocer Henry Kingham & Sons typified the family-run shops lining both sides of the High Street in the early twentieth century. When this staff photograph was taken before the First World War, Kingham employed a young Edwin Ware, who then lived next door and became Pinner's leading historian.

In about 1950 Kingham's neighbour at no. 11 – in a notably attractive sixteenth-century building – was the aptly named Old Oak Tea Rooms. In the previous century it had been the workshop of the Bedford family who were tailors. In later years, Edwin Ware also recalled that the front room of no. 11 was used as a meeting place for Pinner Parish Council.

Given that the High Street has become something of a tourist attraction, it is no surprise that restaurants currently occupy both no. 11 and no. 13. The former now boasts two brass plaques, one commemorating Edwin Ware, the other honouring two members of the Bedford family. The three men were successively parish clerks for close on one hundred years.

In this highly evocative reminder of the High Street from about a hundred years ago, post office staff pose outside no. 23, one of nine different addresses which, at various times, housed the local postal service. In 1932 a custom-built post office was opened in Bridge Street, where it remains to this day.

Like several of its neighbours no. 7 bears a fairly arbitrary date (1721), although this may have been the year the original timber-framed building gained its present brick frontage. What is certain is that it has been occupied over some 120 years by a succession of butchers. In 1968 it was E.G. Brett & Son.

In 2002 the butcher has been replaced by an antiques and collectables centre, but many signs of his trade remain. Those who know where to look can still see a wooden canopy, iron ventilation grilles and an external iron rail with hooks for hanging joints. The name of a past butcher (J.E. Lee) is also incised below the main window.

For the best part of a century Woodmans was one of the great trading names of Pinner. Originally in business as corn chandlers, the firm later moved into garden supplies and by 1920 had this well-stocked shop at no. 19.

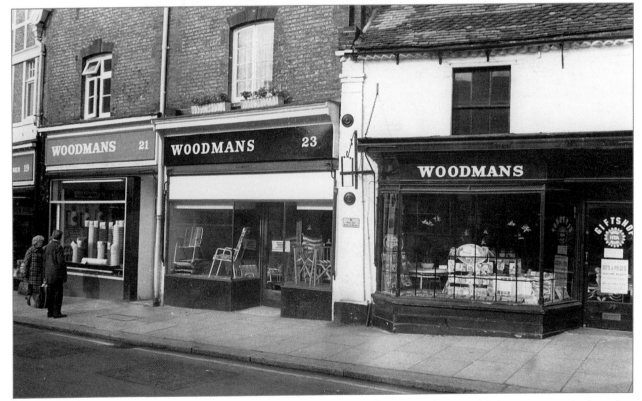

In a district well supplied with house-proud property owners, Woodmans wisely moved into every aspect of garden care and soon had several adjoining shops in the High Street. At the rear they created an early version of today's ubiquitous garden centres.

Commercial pressures to develop the High Street intensified in the late twentieth century, reaching its nadir in 1966 with plans to build a seven-storey block and shopping precinct. Ultimately, two supermarkets were accommodated in the area by cutting through existing shops on either side of the street. The first such passageway was made beneath this 1860s building in the late 1970s.

For all the pretensions of its name Bishops Walk today is a corridor of small shops and businesses. Though the name seemingly evokes that period when archbishops of Canterbury held court nearby, the walk is more prosaically named after Bishops Stores, the first major retailer on the site.

Bishops were later succeeded by Marks & Spencer food hall, at the time (in 1987), the first of its kind to be opened by the company. Currently its landscaping does much to allay the earlier fears expressed by the Pinner Association that 'the dream of a riverside walk would not be entirely shattered'.

With space already found for one supermarket off one side of the High Street, it was inevitable that something similar would be attempted on the other side. In the early 1980s this entrance way was created by carving a passage through the existing no. 16 to a new Sainsburys store on the old Pinner Metropolitan station car park. The modest scale of this passage, however, gives little indication of the vastness of the whole controversial project.

Called Barter's Walk (after a previous owner of the property), this now twenty-year-old passage leads to the main superstore. Massive even by present-day standards, it offers its customers a sales area reported to be fifteen times larger than an earlier Sainsburys shops in nearby Bridge Street.

What proved to be Pinner's biggest controversy began when Sainsbury's and London Transport made a joint application to develop the Metropolitan Line car park. Today the old station building is almost completely dwarfed by its busy commercial neighbour.

Though perhaps not 'the end of Pinner as we know it' (to quote the 1982 fears of the local MP, Sir John Page), the completed development has undoubtedly changed the approach to Pinner for those travelling by train. Even after twenty years, the solid wall of brick (right) suggests arrival in a new town rather than an old village.

2
St John's & its Environs

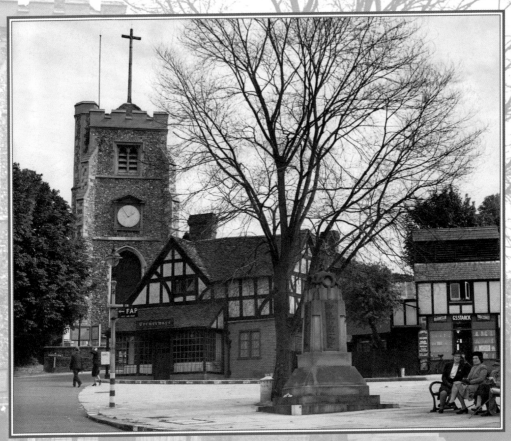

For some eighty years the immediate vicinity of St John's parish church has changed very little, the church, restaurant, 'town tree' and war memorial remaining in harmonious conjunction. This photograph was taken during the Second World War, a date confirmed by the First Aid Post sign (to the left of the war memorial) and, possibly by the hats, gloves and sturdy shoes of the ladies seated on the right. The less-than-flourishing tree was replaced with a species of maple by the ever-generous Pinner Association in 1946.

In common with many other surviving medieval churches, St John's has evolved over the centuries, although its twenty-first-century appearance was clearly established by the time this engraving was made by Samuel Woodburn in 1807. Showing the aspect from Paines Lane, the picture was originally published in a collection of *One Hundred Views of Churches in the Environs of London*.

Approximately a century later, a comparable view of St John's from Paines Lane has gained a few more buildings, notably the Cocoa Tree Coffee Tavern (right). East House Fields (just out of view on the left) was later used as the site of today's Paines Close.

The Loudon Monument, Pinner's most unusual memorial, dominates this view of St John's from Church Lane, *c.* 1910. The pyramid-shaped structure in memory of William and Agnes Loudon, parents of the noted agriculturalist John Claudius Loudon, features what appears to be a coffin suspended in mid-air.

Although over ninety years separate this contemporary view of St John's from the picture above, the only major difference is the acquisition of a lych gate erected in honour of residents who served in the First World War. The Loudon Monument continues to fascinate visitors who often suppose the Loudons to be buried in the mid-air coffin rather than the vault beneath.

Said to equal the height of the chancel, the oak cross on top of St John's tower was once surmounted by a weather vane which blew down in 1878 and was never replaced. This view from Church Lane, taken in 1892, also shows the pretty Chestnut Cottage (which still survives) and the rambling eighteen-room vicarage that was rebuilt further down the lane in the 1930s.

St John's provides a timeless backdrop to this vignette of village life on a winter's day, 1925. Despite the snow a local van driver stops to chat with a delivery man from the Harrow branch of Sainsburys, which had already been trading for around a quarter of a century.

Since the time of Queen Victoria's accession in 1837 there has been a 'town tree' outside St John's. Six years after this picture was taken in about 1892, the tree fell in the night. Its replacement had a relatively short life and was itself replaced by the maple donated by the Pinner Association in 1946.

Today the same view embraces not only a healthy tree but also buildings either side that have survived with their external appearance virtually unchanged. The one-time Cocoa Tree Coffee Tavern on the left has been converted into offices, the butcher's shop (right) is once again a restaurant, as it was in the 1940s.

A rare picture of the St John's end of the High Street taken from behind the town tree, *c.* 1920. It shows William Ashby's timber yard, the barn used by Odells (plumber and decorator) and the early shops and cottages. All were demolished in the building of Grange Court in the early 1930s.

The great louvered ventilation box that caps this building in Church Lane reminds us of its earlier use as an abbatoir for the shop on the left (maintained as a butcher's shop from the time of Oliver Cromwell until the 1930s). Though both premises date from the sixteenth century, the exterior timbering is a twentieth-century fake.

Pinner residents crowd the doors and windows of Grange Court to watch the 'launch' of the fund-raising 'HMS Pinner' during Warship Week, 1942. Sixty years later, with its mixture of flats, businesses and shops, Grange Court remains the biggest and boldest development in the High Street.

In 1970 Sir John Page, then the local MP, opened the High Street Improvement Scheme which brought small but significant alterations to the St John's end of the High Street. Particularly welcome was a well designed and partially enclosed seating area around the village war memorial, for which seats were donated by local Townswomen's Guilds.

For centuries Church Farm was just that – the farm opposite the church with a range of outbuildings that included a sizeable barn (left). In 1900 it became a private residence and has since been home to, among others, Bert Thomas the famous cartoonist of two world wars.

Today's Church Farm is seen here from the far side of the once-private green given to the village in 1922. In 1970, as part of the High Street Improvement Scheme, the existing fencing was replaced with neat posts and chains and a variety of native trees were planted on the green.

Building News of March 1878 provides this drawing of Equestrian Villa, the house adjoining St John's, Pinner (drawn immediately prior to the villa's reopening as the Cocoa Tree Coffee Tavern). Prime mover in its transformation was Judge William Barber of Barrow Point House, who hoped to woo drinkers away from Pinner's many pubs.

The work of Barber's architects, the popular Arts and Crafts team of Sir Ernest George and Harold Peto, proved highly durable and in 2002 the building survives with remarkable few alterations. Since its days as a temperance tavern, it has had many roles, from local Conservative Club to its present usage as offices.

The Cocoa Tree quickly developed a profitable sideline as a venue for Sunday School outings and similar treats. The biggest were held not on site, but in a field off Eastcote Road (near the present Meadow Road). Here there was ample space for swing-boats and other children's amusements.

By 1895 the Cocoa Tree was being run on modern entrepreneurial lines by A.C. Cross who christened his Eastcote Road field 'Nower Hill Park'. His improvements included the construction of this vast refreshment tent which, according to a contemporary brochure, 'will give shelter to 1,000 persons'.

Previously part of the parish of St Mary's, Harrow on the Hill, St John's did not become a parish in its own right until 1776. Walter Williams, Pinner's first rector (formerly its curate) chose to live not in the modest vicarage provided but in the grand eighteenth-century mansion, Pinner House, in Church Lane. The mansion was still in private ownership when this picture was taken in 1935.

Put up for sale in 1947, Pinner House was purchased by local subscription and a gift from the Nuffield Trust and reopened as an old people's home the following year. Today the extensive wings subsequently added at the rear of the building provide attractive warden-assisted accommodation.

In the 1860s Elmdene, Church Lane (centre, *c.* 1892) was home to Mrs Horatia Ward and her family. Neighbours knew her best as the widow of a Kent clergyman, but she was also the illegitimate daughter of Lord Nelson and Lady Hamilton.

Having lost a son in 1865 and a daughter in 1872 – the latter having been knocked over and killed by a runaway horse in Pinner High Street – Mrs Horatia Ward subsequently moved to the newly built Woodridings Estate in Hatch End. Her Pinner residence, however, remains a family home to this day.

3
Bridge Street & Love Lane

As the principal route between the village and Pinner Green, Pinner Hill and Hertfordshire's towns, Bridge Street has been witness to all kinds of traffic. In 1968 it even saw the newest craze – the Space Hopper! The local press asked none too seriously: 'Could this be the answer to London's congested roads?

Within the passage of 100 years Bridge Street has changed almost beyond recognition. Indeed, the police station (whose gable can be seen in the centre) is the only building to survive from this souvenir of 1902. On the left is a farriers and general smithy run by Gurney & Hilsden, while on the right is the wall of Howard Place.

Thirty years later Bridge Street was fast becoming a major shopping street, although Dears Farm still stands at the top near the police station. As Pinner's own cinema had yet to be built, the advertisement hoardings then promoted films on show at the Embassy Cinema in neighbouring North Harrow.

By the time of George VI's Coronation in 1937, a spectacularly decorated Bridge Street was packed with big-name multiples. Among them was a Sainsburys, whose subsequent move to their current site was to cause much controversy.

Like many other commercial streets in areas where supermarkets exist, Bridge Street survives with a more eclectic mix of traders. The street is now home to betting shops, charity shops, Chinese and Indian restaurants and even a Chinese medical centre.

In 1905 Dears Farm (right) dominated the view down Bridge Street from Elm Park (formerly Elm Common) Road. By then its farming days were long over and the property housed several tenants, a 'cornman' among them. The farm was finally demolished in 1935.

A similar view taken in about 1981 differs remarkably little from today's scene. The female pedestrian in the foreground is walking past the First Church of Christ erected in 1937.

So Well Remembered, the current attraction when this picture of the Langham was taken in 1947, might well serve as an epitaph for what proved to be the village's first and last cinema. At that time it was just one of eighteen movie houses advertising in the local press.

Where Pinner people once went to the movies, they are now more likely to go supermarket shopping or to the gym. Next door (out of the picture) is the main Pinner Post Office, still on the site it has occupied since 1932.

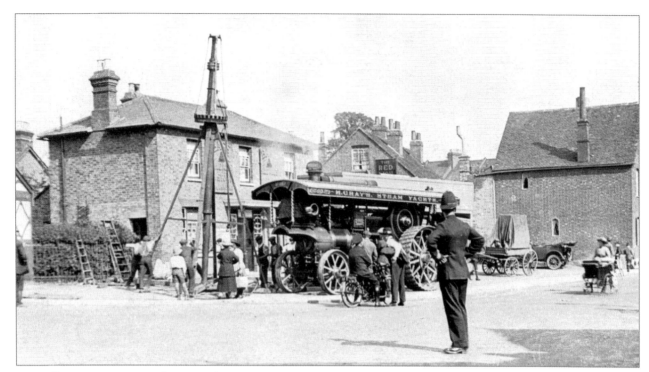

For well over 200 years Bridge Street had its own popular tavern, the Red Lion, seen here on Pinner Fair day in about 1920. On the left can be glimpsed the fire station at the junction with Love Lane and, on the right, a Georgian house demolished in the early 1930s.

Given the broad turning area at the Love Lane junction, the forecourt of the Red Lion was a sensible choice for a bus terminus, initially for this LNWR horse omnibus which ran between Pinner village and Pinner (Hatch End) station.

In spring 1950 buses were still waiting outside the Bridge Street pub, although many locals obviously preferred to use their bicycles. Built on the site of an earlier tavern in 1875, the Red Lion served its last drinks in 1963.

Today the pub name survives in Red Lion Parade (left) built on the same site in 1963. In the centre can be seen the trees of the High Street Memorial Gardens, a tiny green oasis at the junction of three busy roads. It railings are normally covered with posters for the many local events that help to give Pinner a real sense of community.

One of Pinner's oldest thoroughfares, Love Lane may once have been the trackway that enabled the builders of St John's to bring flints from quarries in Waxwell Lane. When photographed in 1882 it was virtually undeveloped and a home to itinerants (right).

By 1903 the Pinner fire station, supported wholly by voluntary subscription, had moved from Waxwell Lane. The lane had also acquired other properties, including (in the distance) Wilby House, now the entrance to a municipal car park. On the left, the horse has just trotted past the gardens of Howard Place.

In 1933 Love Lane's junction with Bridge Street had a branch of the Midland Bank, a butcher's shop and other commercial ventures (left), all housed in a new block designed in the stockbroker-Tudor style increasingly popular at the time.

Almost seventy years later the bank (albeit with a change of name) remains at the corner of a Love Lane that has now distanced itself from its romantic-sounding name. The red-brick bulk of Red Lion Parade (right) also emphasises the present dominance of commercialism.

Although a police station with seven constables, a sergeant and a horse patrol was set up in Pinner in 1840, it was moved two years later to Harrow. A further fifty-seven years were to elapse before a proper station was opened at the top of Bridge Street on ground formerly used as the village pound.

In the twenty-first century Pinner police are still using the same nineteenth-century premises, including the original stables at the rear. The blue lamp outside is also the Victorian original. Owing to staff shortages, the main enquiry office was closed to the public in August 2000, although, at the time of writing, it had reopened recently using a roster of civilian volunteers.

From 1931, for a period of thirty years, St Luke's became the national shrine of St Philomena, a presumed Roman martyr whose skeleton was discovered in catacombs in Rome in 1802. Although originally given Papal approval, the cult of Philomena was ultimately forbidden by a decree of Rome in 1961 after modern research had cast doubts on the authenticity of the remains.

The original church continued to serve the Catholic community throughout the Second World War, but the congregation eventually found the building too small for their needs, so in 1958 a larger church was opened on adjoining ground. Its striking design, featuring deep relief carvings of St Luke and the Virgin Mary, was made by F.X. Velarde, Professor of Architecture at Liverpool University.

Even after the opening of the new St Luke's, the original church remained. In the mid-1960s some parts (including the distinctive polygonal tower to the Love Lane elevation) were successfully incorporated into a new parish centre.

The 1960s also saw the building of a new church hall which, nearly forty years later, retains the dramatically different look much praised in the architectural press of the day. Designed by G.H. and G.P. Grima, it features an imposing full-height entrance porch of toughened glass and an internal circular staircase leading to a spacious gallery.

Until its demolition in 1953 Howard Place provided one of Love Lane's saddest stories. One hundred years earlier, Charlotte Howard had set aside £47,000 to erect twenty-one almshouses for widows of officers and clergymen. When she died her relatives challenged her will, and even though the High Court ruled that her intentions were to be honoured, only sufficient money remained to build these three houses in mock-Tudor style.

4
Along Marsh Road

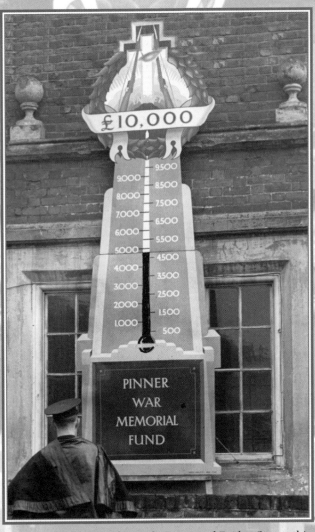

Situated where Marsh Road meets the High Street and Bridge Street, this solid, red-brick building was a local landmark for well over one hundred years. In 1946 it was still serving as Pinner's public hall and was thus an ideal site for the Village War Memorial Fund indicator. Later the same year the building was converted for use as a public library.

The cluster of people gathered at the junction of Marsh Road and High Street in about 1900 may well have been drawn by the sight of one of the first motor cars in the village. To their right is the building that served as Pinner's first National School from 1841 to 1868 before becoming its public hall. Services were held here during the 1879 restoration of the parish church.

The same view in March 1951 reveals a handsome Edwardian building (left), originally designed for Barclays Bank in 1905. The first Victory pub and lock-up shops on the approach to Pinner Metropolitan station can also be seen. By that time the public hall had been converted for use as the municipal library.

Enlarged for Queen Victoria's Jubilee, the old 1840s school building finally became home to a number of small local businesses in the 1950s. Its days were numbered, however, and demolition followed shortly after in 1966.

At the start of the twenty-first century the High Street end of Marsh Road displays a typical marriage of old and new, with the Edwardian corner building having a new office block neighbour, albeit built in a reasonably sympathetic red brick. Between the two there is a courtyard belonging to the Victory pub. The latter has now removed to 4 High Street.

For many decades Marsh Road boasted two public houses – the now-removed Victory and the George – seen here in the early years of the twentieth century. Built in the late 1880s, the George occupied the site of a previous tavern named after George II and first licensed in 1751.

Ever since the Metropolitan Railway came to Pinner in 1885, the George has (literally) been in the shadow of the Marsh Road railway bridge. In 1961 as part of the line's modernisation, a new bridge was rolled into position virtually outside its doors.

Twenty-five years after the construction of the railway bridge the George was hemmed in further by an office block built on its other side. As seen in this contemporary press photograph, the block has a solid steel skeleton which all but dwarfs its neighbour.

After a period as the Frothfinders and Firkin, the George is currently under new management and has returned to its original name. Though the restoration has been widely welcomed, locals have criticised the pub's new neon-lit name sign as well as other promotional additions made to its essentially Victorian façade.

In about 1914 the second Pinner National School shared this lane (now called School Lane) with the early nineteenth-century Lichfield Cottage. Note the pile of bricks in the unmade road which were possibly used in the building of nearby Stanley Villas.

When the village outgrew its first school this handsome replacement was erected only a few minutes' walk from the original building on the opposite side of Marsh Road in 1886. As this photograph, taken in 1915, reveals, the builders made good use of the fancy brickwork so popular at the time.

In 2002 School Lane is a quiet cul-de-sac with a typical mix of twentieth-century suburban properties. Only the name sign reminds us of its former importance in the life of the village.

The River Pinn once ran through the grounds of the Grove, which about a century ago was one of the few buildings of any consequence off Marsh Road. Although the house was demolished in 1950, its name, as indeed that of its most famous resident, lives on in several contemporary place-names.

Grove Lodge currently stands as a reminder of a more opulent past at the junction of Marsh Road and today's Grove Avenue. The adjoining red-brick building served for many years as Pinner's telephone exchange, but is continued use is now under threat.

Most of the original estate of the Grove is now occupied by an estate of a different kind, though it is still called, appropriately enough, the Grove Estate. Built at the beginning of the 1950s, its bulk and unadorned functionalism are all too typical of the immediate post-war era.

Neatly tucked away inside the estate – and within sight of stretches of the River Pinn – now stands a 1970s old people's home. Its name, Milmans, recalls the family name of three generations of owners of the Grove, including Sir Francis Milman, physician to Queen Charlotte, wife of King William IV.

Even older than the Grove was Pinner Place, an early eighteenth-century rebuilding of a far older property fronting on to Marsh Road. Its most famous inhabitants included the crown jeweller James Garrard and John Zephaniah Holwell, survivor and chronicler of the horrors of the Black Hole of Calcutta. The latter is now remembered by Holwell Place, one of the suburban streets subsequently built in the vicinity.

Serving as a hospital during the First World War, Pinner Place survived the Second World War only to be demolished in 1954. That same year, local builder B.H. Cutler began building the semi-detached houses now known as Ashridge Gardens and then described as 'the first post-war private enterprise estate in Harrow'.

Pinner Baptist church was opened at the junction of Marsh Road and Cecil Park in 1885 after the site of their first meeting place in Chapel Lane was required for the building of the railway. In about 1910, the date of this photograph, the Baptists moved again – this time to their present church in Paines Lane.

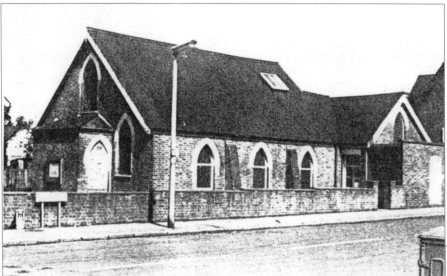

Having had a variety of uses, the old Baptist chapel ultimately became Pinner's first synagogue. It was consecrated in 1951 after High Festival services held in the nearby Vagabonds Hall had attracted enough members of the Jewish faith to warrant securing a proper and permanent place of worship.

In 1981 Pinner Synagogue was rebuilt on the same site to virtually universal acclaim. The architectural press in particular felt that with its pitch roof and brick walls (featuring a relief of the traditional seven-branch candlestick or *menorah*) it fitted neatly into its residential surroundings.

Built by the aptly named Metropolitan Railway Surplus Lands Co. on the south side of their line through Pinner, Cecil Park was already taking shape when this picture was taken in about 1902. Large and airy, these first homes were not dissimilar to the highly regarded Bedford Park development at Chiswick.

Though to contemporary eyes Cecil Park looks much of a piece, subsequent house building was on a more modest scale. Development of the northern half of the Railways Surplus land, including roads such as Grange Gardens, had to await the interwar period.

Taken from a card posted in Hatch End in 1916, this relatively rare view is captioned 'The Marsh Bridge, Pinner'. In the absence of further evidence, it is presumably the footbridge over the River Pinn at the point where it runs under Marsh Road.

Hard to believe that this is the heart of Pinner in 2002! Yet just yards away from this sun-dappled, seemingly woodland scene, is the busy Marsh Road/High Street junction.

5

Towards Eastcote

In the mid-1930s the River Pinn really did look more like a river than the stream which can occasionally be glimpsed on walks around the village today. This was especially true in Cannon Lane off Eastcote Road, where this picture was taken for publication in Walter Druett's 1937 book *Pinner Through the Ages*.

Over the centuries Pinner folk have found that living with even a small river on its doorstep is not without its hazards. Here we see the still rural Eastcote Road connecting the villages of Pinner and Eastcote all but washed away in about 1910. In fact the Pinn was still bursting its banks as late as 1988.

A tamed Pinn is seen in this contemporary shot taken at the first bridge in Eastcote Road. Like its counterpart in nearby Cannon Lane, this bridge has both a name and a history, being called Milman's bridge after the Milman family who lived at the Grove.

Cannon Lane has had a succession of bridges over the Pinn for many hundreds of years. The crossing shown here in 1930 was itself a replacement of an earlier bridge which had been 'rebuilt from the foundation' in 1728 at the expense of Grace, Lady Hunsden, who as a girl lived at Pinner Hill.

The Hunsden bridge exists even to this day, although it is unlikely that many motorists or, for that matter, pedestrians, ever notice it. The commemorative plaque of 1728, now barely readable, has been remounted on the wall at almost pavement level.

Nursemaids pause to chat in this evocative shot of Cannon Lane as it looked in Edwardian times when the first few family homes were already occupied. Even then the road was an old highway, which, according to Pinner historian Edwin Ware, may once have housed an early religious foundation.

Despite some twentieth-century additions, these Edwardian houses are still recognisable today. Edwin Ware's research into the area led him to believe that the proper spelling of the name of the road is Canon, as in canon law. An alternative derivation stems from one John Canoun, who was listed in the Middlesex Records of 1782.

For decades the most substantial building in Cannon Lane was Downs Farm. The road was known for a while as Princes Lane, after a Mr Prince who farmed there. In 1956 the farm was taken over by the Methodists who had been a presence in the village since the very early nineteenth century.

In 1965 the Methodists began building the present handsome church. Local Methodists also currently attend the 1937 church at the junction of Love Lane and Avenue Road.

Had the cart driver on the left of this 1906 view been a stranger to Pinner, the signpost in the middle of the junction of Eastcote Road and Marsh Road would have pointed him safely in the right direction. As it clearly shows, the right fork would have taken him to Eastcote, Ruislip and Uxbridge.

Over ninety years later the same houses still stand on the same corner. The traffic lights and road markings now indicate just how busy the junction has become.

For all its modest appearance the Vagabonds Hall in Eastcote Road, near its Marsh Road junction, was for decades one of the premier assembly halls in the district and home to the amateur dramatic group the Vagabond Players. It was demolished in the 1970s.

The site of the Vagabonds Hall is still much visited in the twenty-first century, for it now houses the Pinner Medical Centre. The name 'vagabonds' seemingly refers to a somewhat bohemian element of the old Pinner Men's Club which broke away from the more conventional parent body in 1920.

Pinner's outskirts were still largely under grass when this picture was taken in 1932, roughly at the point where Rayners Lane meets today's Whittington Way and Suffolk Road. Of the two visible directional signs (right), the lower points the way across the fields to North Harrow station.

Exactly seventy years later the homes advertised on the hoardings shown in the picture above – and many more besides – have all been built. Nevertheless a few green trees and verges remain among the clutter of street furniture essential to twenty-first century transportation.

6

Some old Pinner Lanes

Drawn from a viewpoint in Chapel Lane by an unknown artist, this charming study shows the late nineteenth-century village quietly going about its daily business, *c.* 1884. Most of its features have long since disappeared, including the wooden cottages on either side of the lane and the hump-backed bridge (centre, right) which then crossed the River Pinn.

In about 1900 the view across Bridge Street to Chapel Lane still embraced a row of wooden cottages immediately in front of the railway embankment (from which smoke from a passing train can just be seen). Higher up the lane a similar cottage housed the first Methodist meetings which led to the creation of a small chapel nearby.

For some years before and after the First World War, the shop at the right-hand corner of Chapel Lane sold newspapers, cigarettes and confectionery, G. Jaques (shown here) being succeeded by Brewsters. At this time, small traders also occupied the cottages on the left.

Today all that remains of the earlier lane is a rebuilt and widened railway bridge and the house (left), currently occupied by an estate agent. Police concern about possible drug dealing recently saw the closure of the public conveniences near the bridge.

Set at an angle of Chapel Lane with West End Lane, the mansion now known as West House was once considered one of the glories of Pinner, and could be yet again if conservationists have their way. This picture was taken by its head gardener in 1933 when the house was owned by Mr J.S. Hogg, chairman of the Gore Division of magistrates.

Purchased by Pinner residents as a village war memorial in 1947, the actual upkeep of West House proved beyond the resources of the local authority to whom it was subsequently given. Today the lake and grounds are still much visited, but what remains of the house has fallen victim to both the passage of time and vandals.

Contemporary visitors are quickly made aware of the existence of a West House Appeal through which the Pinner Association has already raised nearly £100,000 towards the restoration of the house. It is hoped it will then be used as a showcase for original artwork, books and ephemera connected with the life and career of Pinner's popular humourist and artist, William Heath Robinson.

Today the original West House Estate and what was once the adjoining Bennett's Park have been merged to form the Pinner War Memorial Park. Just a few feet from its Chapel Lane entrance, a plaque set in the walkway reminds passers by of its dedication to the memory of the fallen of two world wars.

Running more or less straight from
the top of Bridge Street to the
Pinner Green end of Uxbridge
Road, Waxwell Lane is one of the
district's most intriguing
thoroughfares, not least because
the name stems from a well which
is still in existence. Seen here with
a small boy perched on top in
about 1890, the Wax Well was
once an important source of water
for the area. As such, it was much
used until the late nineteenth
century.

Now set in the middle of a well-tended green, the original well-head has become something of a tourist attraction and
bears a plaque donated by the Harrow Heritage Trust. The water from the well was once considered especially
beneficial to those suffering from complaints of the eye.

By 1921 substantial houses already lined the right-hand side of Waxwell Lane at its junction with Love Lane. Nevertheless, the rough road surface with its horse-drawn carts still gave it the atmosphere of a country lane.

Almost eighty years later the junction retains much of its original leafy look and Waxwell Lane remains pleasant for walkers. At the same time, the sheer number of motorists using the area has led to the introduction of extensive traffic-calming measures.

Even in a district rich in pubs with fascinating histories, the Oddfellows Arms in Waxwell Lane stands out. Built in 1853 by a member of one of Pinner's best-known families, the Ellements, it was largely financed by money from the local friendly society – the Manchester Unity of the Independent Order of Oddfellows.

Happily both pub and adjoining cottages have survived into the twenty-first century. While the ground floor of the Oddfellows has been reconstructed over the years, its façade retains the sturdy cottage look of the original building.

Six terraced cottages were originally built next door to the pub by local labour and given the name Unity Place. In the late 1940s, their occupants were among those receiving meals on wheels. This vital role was carried out by the local Women's Voluntary Service, using a van donated by American friends in Boston, Massachusetts.

Apart from the odd television aerial the cottages look much as they did in the nineteenth century. The plaque identifying the row as Unity Place has disappeared over the years.

Oakfield School in Paines Lane was run by the Misses Thompson, the daughters of a naval officer's widow then living at Howard Place. In the decades before and after the First World War, the school educated the children of local gentry producing among other successful scholars, a future headmaster of Harrow School.

Like so much of early twentieth-century Pinner, Oakfield School ultimately made way for the kind of substantial private residences that have since made the area a highly desirable place to live. Only recently the local press quoted a resident's view that 'just being called Pinner adds another £5,000 on your property'.

Another early Paines Lane property was Weatherley's Farm, named after a Weatherley who, according to Edwin Ware, appears in the Rate Books for 1859. The house was subsequently acquired by the influential Judge William Barber of Barrow Point House, who rebuilt it as Oakfield School.

Probably the Pynes Lane mentioned in medieval Court Rolls, Paines Lane has long been a vital link between the village and Uxbridge Road. Its early properties included these attractive cottages on the site of today's nos 91 to 93. In 1909, the year of this picture, they were already seventy years old.

Waxwell Lane's Bee Cottage (dating in part from 1590) is probably lucky to have survived, as it became so dilapidated in the 1960s that the local authority came close to ordering its demolition. Happily, after effective lobbying by the Pinner Association, grants were obtained for its restoration to the attractive home it is in 2002.

Pinner's Victorian past is still vividly evoked in Paines Lane cemetery whose two acres of land was purchased in about 1856 for the goodly sum of £200 an acre. Efforts to buy ground closer to the existing churchyard had previously failed. The cemetery was consecrated in August 1859.

This simple flat stone marks the Paines Lane grave of Horatia Ward, illegitimate daughter of Lord Nelson, who died in 1881. She had come to Pinner after the death of her clergyman husband. The inscription acknowledges her famous father but makes no reference to her equally famous mother, Lady Hamilton.

The Pierce family outside the picturesque creeper-covered Gardener's Cottage that stood in Barrow Point Lane, *c.* 1912. The unusual name of Barrow Point may be derived from a tumulus said to have been uncovered in the area.

Right: From 1870 Barrow Point House, off Paines Lane, stood at the heart of a considerable estate belonging to Judge William Barber whose generosity, as we have seen, gave the village both the Cocoa Tree Tavern and Oakfield School. Some eleven years after this pleasing group was photographed in 1913, the house became home to St John's Preparatory School for Boys. Despite the main house being almost destroyed by fire in 1930, the school remained on the site until 1970.

In 2002 the name is remembered in the comparatively recent Barrowdene Close, pictured here, as well as in the firmly established Barrow Point Avenue and Barrow Point Lane. In 1970 St John's School moved to nearby Potter Street Hill.

Extending almost from North Harrow to Hatch End, Moss Lane has so many twists and turns that Pinner historian Edwin Ware believed its name might have derived from *maes* – an Old English word for maze! At its heart, in what is now a private cul-de-sac, remain some of the village's oldest buildings still looking very much as they do in this photograph from about 1908. The house in the centre is East End Farm Cottage which remained a farmhouse until the mid-1930s. Next door, East End House was once home to the largely forgotten Henry James Pye, Poet Laureate to King George III.

The Fives Court in Moss Lane takes its name from the court built at the rear of the property and shown here in a 1909 illustration from a book called *Modern Homes*. The house was designed by the Arts and Crafts architect Cecil Brewer for his cousin Ambrose (later Sir Ambrose) Heal of the famous Tottenham Court Road furnishing store.

Still one of the district's most charming family homes, the Fives Court, seen here from Wakehams Hill, retains virtually all its original features and is now Grade II listed. As early as 1908 it was extended at the rear to accommodate the fast-growing Heal family.

Long before the Fives Court was built for Ambrose Heal Jnr, his father – another Ambrose – had bought this old farmhouse to which the architectural practice of Smith and Brewer made considerable alterations in 1895. Called Nower Hill House, the property was demolished in 1963.

Nower Hill House before Heal's extensions is seen in the background of this view of the Tooke Memorial fountain, *c.* 1892, honouring one of Pinner's great Victorian benefactors, William Tooke. For decades the memorial has been surrounded by a large open space, widely known as Tooke's Green.

Although the fountain itself is no longer in working order and the green is overlooked by typical twentieth-century houses, Tooke's Memorial still stands 116 years after it was erected. Over the years the Pinner Association as well as public-spirited individuals have donated a number of bench seats to the green, enabling strollers to pause and admire a still-pleasing scene.

Nower Hill, the name originally given by Ambrose Heal Snr to his house, was later applied to the whole section of the highway linking Pinner Road with Moss Lane. This picture of the junction is undated; however, because of the blacked-out lamp on the central island, it is presumed to have been taken during the First World War.

Over eighty years later the Pinner Road/Nower Hill junction still has the same houses on the right-hand side, although they have since been joined by many more similar homes. The central island has also been greatly expanded as befits an era of cars rather than carts.

The Hall, an elegant mansion off Paines Lane, was once home to Jessie Bird, who married Nelson Ward, grandson of the great naval hero. Later, in Victorian and Edwardian days, the Nugent family made it the centre of Pinner social life with events that ranged from summer flower shows to winter skating parties on its lake.

Principal access to the Hall was from the Uxbridge Road where the entrance lodge stands to this day. The original twin gateposts now flank the approach to a modern road aptly called Old Hall Drive.

In this undated (but probably Edwardian) photograph taken in the grounds of the Hall, two smartly dressed men admire the view from the rustic bridge over the Pinn. Its waters then fed the Hall's lake.

Though for the most part controlled and culverted, the Pinn makes an occasional appearance in some of the streets subsequently built on the Hall's estate. Access to some homes in Moss Close, for example, can only be gained by way of individual bridges.

Wakehams Hill, which climbs steeply from Moss Lane to run parallel with the vast open spaces of Pinner Park Farm, is named after the cobbler who occupied this little cottage in the last decade of the nineteenth century. The cottage was probably built as a lodge to Pinner Park, and was demolished in 1971.

In 2002 a viewpoint over farmland still exists roughly where the cottage once stood. Sadly, the pleasure to be had from sitting on the seats, donated by the Pinner comedienne Molly Weir among others, is somewhat diminished by the quantities of rubbish regularly dumped there.

7

A Pinner Miscellany

The annual fair in the streets of Pinner has brought a fame that extends well beyond the village boundaries, not least because it appears to have been held without interruption every year since 1336 – and possibly for some years before that. The pattern of more recent times, when fairground attractions pack the High Street, was already set at the time this unusual picture was taken from the tower of St John's in the 1930s.

Nobody can be entirely sure how many fairs had preceded this one in 1885, because experts now believe the fair's charter, originally granted 'to Pynnore' by King Edward III, merely confirmed an already existing event.

Since 1900, when this view up the High Street was taken, the fair has changed surprisingly little, except for the date of its celebration. Originally held to mark the June birthday of St John the Baptist, the date was subsequently brought forward to the Wednesday of Whitsun week.

As the fair grew in popularity, its attractions took over more and more of the streets of Pinner, including Bridge Street, seen here early in the twentieth century. For this reason various attempts have been made over the years to either relocate it to a more convenient space or abolish it entirely.

In this 1929 view looking down the High Street, many of the showmen are occupying their regular pitches. The Pettigrove family, for example, ran a series of carousels pitched in front of the church for over a century.

'Pay here' says the neon-lit kiosk – and pay the punters certainly did in 2002 – up to £2.50 a ride, even during the middle of the day when prices are traditionally cheaper. A far cry from the 6d and 1s treats of my youth!

In 2002 Pinner Fair offered amusements of a scale and size unimaginable a century before, with many of the installations (such as these erected in Bridge Street) rising well above the surrounding rooftops. Despite damp and unseasonable weather and a change of date (to avoid clashes with Golden Jubilee celebrations), it still attracted the crowds from morning to night.

It is not just the fairground attractions that have moved with the times – so too have the showmen. Where once they arrived in horse-drawn gypsy caravans, Fair Day 2002 saw the Chapel Lane car park packed with the sleekest of mobile homes.

One of the best-kept secrets of contemporary Pinner is the existence of a veritable network of chalk mines beneath an area roughly bordered by Uxbridge Road at its Pinner Green end and Norman Crescent. As this *Harrow Observer* photograph (right) from 1970 reveals, many of the mine galleries reach a height of at least twice that of an average man. Mining in Pinner seems to have died out after 1870 when it was cheaper to transport chalk and lime from the Chilterns via the newly expanded railway system.

Although the mines are said to be in a remarkable state of preservation, all entrances are currently sealed in the interests of safety. The most prominent entrance can be found in a coppice off the Uxbridge Road's Montesole Playing Fields, where a heavy manhole cover is enclosed in a vandal-proof metal cage.

Pinner's generous spread of centuries-old pubs extends to Pinner Green where drinkers have frequented the Bell since 1751. Although no illustration seems to have survived of the first Bell, the second Bell, shown here, was built between 1830 and 1835 on the site of today's Bell Close.

For thirty years the Bell was a scheduled stop for the Pinner horse bus which ran six times a day every weekday from the Cocoa Tree at the top of the High Street to Hatch End station. Driver George Bridge made his last journey in 1914 before becoming a ticket collector at Hatch End station.

In about 1890 the Bell boasted continental-style shutters to its downstairs windows. Licensee Austin Carley was no less proud of his Stanhope gig, shown here with farmer Gregory of Woodhall Farm holding the reins.

Since 1931, when it was rebuilt in the then fashionable road-house style, the Bell has occupied a prominent position at the junction of Elm Park Road and Pinner Green. Following recent trends, it has now changed its traditional name to the Orange Tree.

In 1880 an unknown artist painted this charming souvenir of the days when Pinner village had its own windmill. Once the central feature of Mill Farm off Pinner Hill Road, the mill's origins are unclear, although it is known to have been of a type widely seen in the early seventeenth century.

Mill Farm Cottages which once adjoined Pinner's mill are seen here in about 1914 from the invaluable Edwin Ware 'Pinner in the Vale' collection. In its later years, the mill was used only for grinding animal meal.

As shown by this press cutting of 1976, Mill Farm Cottages survived – albeit in a derelict state – until the last quarter of the twentieth century. Now, however, all traces of both cottages and farm have disappeared, though the name itself is perpetuated in the present-day Mill Farm Close.

With its highly anonymous mid-twentieth-century buildings, Mill Farm Close gives no hint of the area's picturesque past. The nearby railway workers' homes, Coronation Cottages, which were so small that they were known locally as the 'rabbit hutches', have vanished without trace.

Arthur Tooke of the philanthropic Victorian family whose charity is commemorated by Tooke's Green, is also remembered for his fascination with ornamental towers. In all, Tooke erected three separate towers in different parts of Pinner, including this clock tower dating from 1862, part of a stable block at Pinner Hill Farm. When this photograph was taken in 1976, the clock tower was in visible need of repair.

Though there may be some doubt about the date of this view of Pinner Hill Farm (though possibly 1940s), there is no doubt about the point from which it was taken – the top of Tooke's Tower. The view also shows how the farm, once the home farm of Pinner Hill House, was already being surrounded by suburban housing.

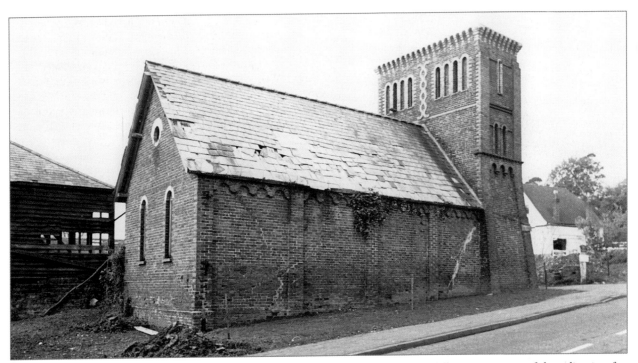

By 1980 Tooke's Tower at Pinner Hill Farm had lost its roof and clock. Happily, following a successful application for change of use, the whole block was sympathetically restored. A plaque dated 1985 records the valuable contributions made by several local businesses as well as by bodies such as Harrow Council and the Pinner Association.

One hundred and forty years after its construction, Tooke's Tower remains among the district's most distinctive landmarks. To this day it retains a low enclosing wall made from original stone sleepers used in the building of the London and Birmingham Railway's line through Harrow in 1837. They were discarded when wooden sleepers were judged to be more efficient.

Though some old photograph captions dub the tower at Pinner Hill Farm 'Tooke's Folly', the name was originally coined for an even more grandiose product of the same lively imagination. This was Woodhall Towers, built in 1864 and adjoining Woodhall Farm which Tooke also owned. His folly, seen here in 1934, was said to have been inspired by a château which Tooke had admired on his travels through Europe.

Pinner Hill House was at one time home to Arthur Tooke and the setting for the third of his Pinner towers. Sadly, it was subsequently judged to be unsafe and pulled down. The original eighteenth-century house to which Tooke added this extravagant neo-Gothic façade now serves as the clubhouse of Pinner Hill Golf Club.

It would have been foolishly optimistic to expect any replacement for Woodhall Towers to match its originality – and so it proved! When the estate was auctioned in 1965, planning permission was obtained for thirty detached homes of which this contemporary picture gives a glimpse. Only one link to the past remains – this street is called Tooke Close.

8

Hatch End

George Bridge, one-time driver of the Pinner horse bus, is seen here in his subsequent role as Hatch End station's ticket collector, in 1914, as indicated by the poster behind him which refers to cheap railway excursions for Easter that year.

Having seen the benefits neighbouring Harrow had derived from the advent of the railway in 1837, Pinner residents were soon pressing for a railway stop in their area. Within five years, a station initially called Pinner, seen here towards the end of the nineteenth century, was opened near the Dove House bridge on the Uxbridge Road.

Opposite: In 1911 Hatch End station was redesigned by Gerald Horsley, an architect whose reputation has grown with the years. Today the station is a listed building, described in a recent railway heritage book as 'a little gem'. Horsley's rebuilding work in Harrow and Wealdstone station is also much-admired.

When this photograph of the station was taken in March 1912, only two travellers were waiting on the 'fast' platform. By then, the station had been more accurately christened Pinner and Hatch End, an acknowledgement of the fact that Pinner village was actually 1½ miles away.

For much of the nineteenth and early twentieth century, post office facilities existed at Hatch End station, at first in the stationmaster's house, and subsequently in the single-storey building nearest the camera in this pre-1911 view. Look very closely and you may just glimpse a telegraph boy with his bicycle behind the wooden fence.

Today a considerably wider bridge is bare of structures other than the familiar British Rail logo. A sub-post office currently occupies 407 Uxbridge Road, following the closure of a larger office in the same road in 1991.

Woodridings Farm, *c*. 1904. The farm was well-known for the quality of its milk which was delivered to the door in the churn. The small float (right) promises 'special cows kept for nursery and invalids'. Woodridings, meaning the clearing in the wood, has been found on a lease of 1445.

Woodridings Farm was demolished in 1950, but the name currently survives in Woodridings Close, a pleasant residential cul-de-sac off Uxbridge Road. The present-day Hatch End Broadway was also largely built on what had previously been farmland.

Although the chantry chapel of St Mary's, Harrow on the Hill, was endowed with land at Hatch End as long ago as 1324, the present community only began to emerge after the railway station had been opened in 1842. This was followed a decade or so later by the building of the nearby Woodridings Estate. Among the estate's first tenants were the young London-based publisher Samuel Beeton, who saw Hatch End as the ideal home for himself and his bride-to-be, Isabella. Within years of her arrival, she had won enduring fame as cookery and household management expert Mrs Beeton.

Mrs Beeton's Hatch End home, 2 Chandos Villas, is seen as it originally appeared in the prospectus for the Woodridings Estate printed in 1855. Here she wrote much of her famous *Book of Household Management*. A footnote recalls that in 1857 she produced 'a useful soup' which was given to the poor of the district.

Appropriately enough the presumed site of 2 Chandos Villas is now a restaurant in Hatch End Broadway. Since 1997 its façade has borne a plaque, given by the Harrow Heritage Trust, commemorating the achievements of a woman who died tragically young after the birth of her fourth child.

Of the fifty or so villas on the Woodridings Estate only these properties, now 40 and 42 Wellington Road, remain – albeit somewhat changed from the original homes. In addition to Mrs Beeton, the estate can claim among its former residents, the writer Ivy Compton Burnett (who lived here as a child) and the poet A.E. Housman.

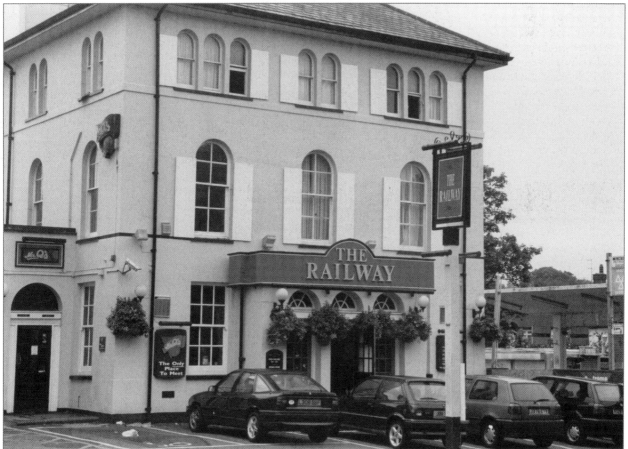

To complete the estate, both a church and a tavern were built. The former, little more than a tin tabernacle, was later replaced by the present St Anselm's. Under the name of the Railway, the tavern still trades in Hatch End Broadway.

St Anselm's Church, completed in time for consecration in June 1895, was a Victorian flint and red-brick edifice costing some £3,449, tucked away in the quiet Westfield Park, off Uxbridge Road. A little more than a decade later a new aisle and vestries were added, the former to accommodate pupils of the nearby Commercial Travellers School.

Opposite: A parish church in its own right since 1902, St Anselm's now shares Westfield Park with a number of more modern properties. The church's most unusual interior feature is its rood screen installed against the opposition of many who found it idolatrous.

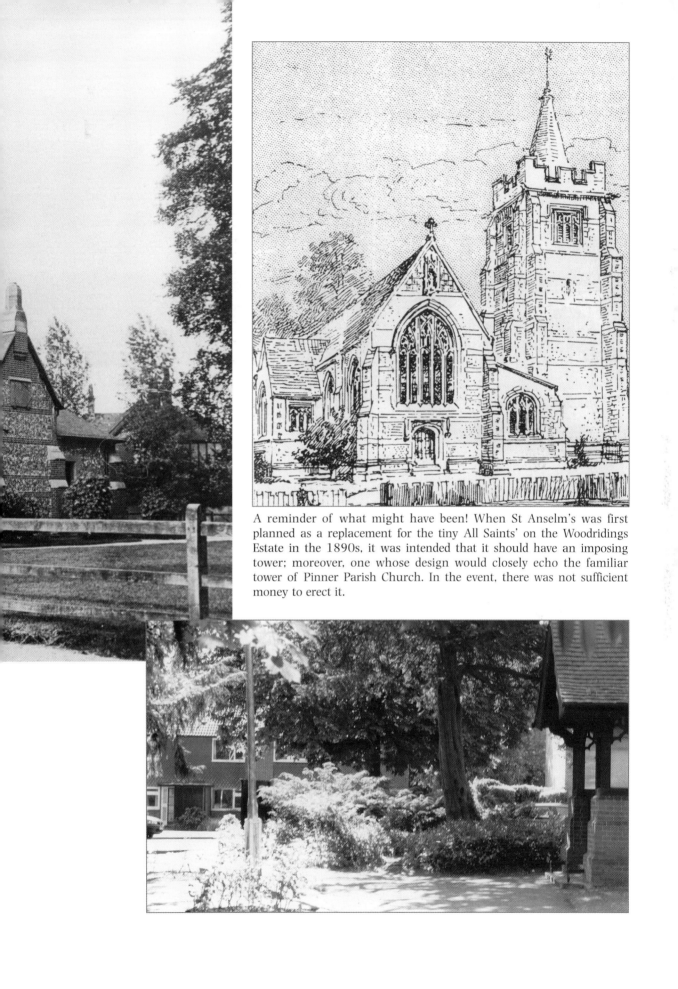

A reminder of what might have been! When St Anselm's was first planned as a replacement for the tiny All Saints' on the Woodridings Estate in the 1890s, it was intended that it should have an imposing tower; moreover, one whose design would closely echo the familiar tower of Pinner Parish Church. In the event, there was not sufficient money to erect it.

Woodhall Farm, shown here in a lithograph of 1810, took its name from the medieval Manor of Woodhall. In about 1807, its buildings and some 358 acres were leased by the noted agriculturalist John Claudius Loudon, who used it as a base from which to pioneer many of the farming methods that were to make his name.

Having described the original farmhouse as a 'large, comfortless, ill-arranged dwelling', Loudon set about redesigning it. The pleasing result survives today – but as a private residence.

During the 1930s much of the land surrounding the farmhouse was bought for development which included the pleasant Woodhall Gate. Then, as now, its homes look out on a kind of village green, which in May 1945 was the scene of this children's party celebrating VE Day.

Today Loudon and his era are evoked by the neighbouring property called the Loudon House. This is, in fact, a twentieth-century creation, deliberately and gracefully built to compliment the genuine Woodhall Farm next door. At the time it was commended in the annual design awards sponsored by the Harrow Heritage Trust and the *Harrow Observer*.

The milk float travelling down an otherwise empty Royston Park Road, *c.* 1920, almost certainly belonged to Woodridings Farm. Among the farm's more popular products was the oddly-named Pinner Lactic Cheese, subsequently produced by the much larger St Ivel Co.

In comparison with the picture above, both sides of Royston Park Road now present an unbroken row of pleasant homes, of which the earliest date from 1893. Further building followed in 1900 and after 1913, giving the road an air of early twentieth-century comfort and solidity.

To those of a literary bent, Pinnerwood House, seen here in 1929, is best known as the residence in which Edward Bulwer-Lytton wrote *Eugene Aram*. Lytton, who was later to inherit the palatial Knebworth House over the border in Hertfordshire, rented the Pinner property in 1831.

Little changed, Pinnerwood House survives today as part of an interesting group of buildings that includes the still-working Pinnerwood Farm and Stud, Pinnerwood Cottage and Pinnerwood Lodge, all situated in this quiet, private road off Woodhall Drive. Its isolation was once protected by a notice reading 'Every third person passing through this farm will be shot'!

In this 1855 press illustration, Prince Albert, Consort to Queen Victoria, is seen arriving for the opening of the Commercial (later the Royal Commercial) Travellers' School, which had been built on land acquired but never used by the railway. The prince made most of his journey by train but, unhappily for the railway authorities, his train was twenty minutes late!

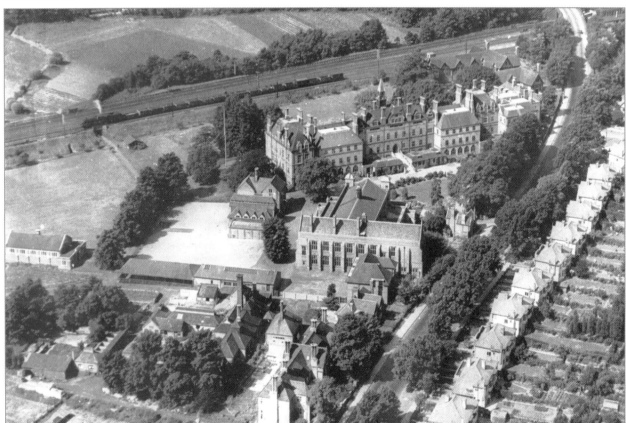

As revealed in this 1947 aerial photograph the school packed a number of impressive buildings on to a triangular site bordered by the railway (top) and Uxbridge Road (right). Originally planned as a school for orphans, it subsequently provided education for any child whose parent was a commercial traveller.

Most impressive of the school's buildings was the great assembly hall, now known as the Elliott Hall. Built at considerable cost in 1905, it provided the ideal setting for major school events such as this undated (but probably Edwardian) speech day.

On possibly the same occasion featured above, a crocodile of small boys, identically clad in jumpers, knickerbockers and boots, files past the hall, perhaps to the sound of the brass band (right of centre). According to historian Edwin Ware 'one of the sights of Pinner' was to see the children marched to spend their pocket money.

Since the late 1980s the Elliott Hall, the only major building to survive the school's closure in 1963, has served as the Harrow Art Centre. In an area woefully short of performance spaces, this venue is regularly used for musical and theatrical performances.

In 1991 much of the original school land was used to house a Safeway supermarket after an even bigger Sainsbury's project had been refused on the grounds that it encroached on green belt land. At night, Safeway now provides an overflow car park for patrons of the adjoining hall (left).

9
Headstone

Headstone, the district that adjoins Hatch End, takes its name from its oldest property, Headstone Manor. It was already thirty years old when it was acquired as a residence for the then Archbishop of Canterbury (and Lord of the Manor of Harrow) in 1344. From medieval times until the early 1920s (the date of this photograph), it was worked as a farm and important ancillary farm structures survive to the present day. Together they make up one of the most interesting groups of buildings in Middlesex and form an apt setting for the Harrow Museum and Heritage Centre.

The Manor House, seen here in an engraving of 1800, has survived as a mixture of many periods, the earliest being 1501, according to a date inscribed on one of its bricks. To this day the moat remains filled with water, but the strange topiary giant (far right) has long since disappeared.

A glimpse of the bridge that crosses the moat can be seen (right) in this 1925 view which also shows the estate's magnificent Tudor barn (left) which stands approximately 31ft tall and 151ft long. Its doors were obviously built to a height that would allow easy access to even the most fully-loaded wagon.

In public use since the 1920s, Headstone Manor was later the focus of a vast and costly restoration programme, of which the first phase was completed in 1973. A celebratory barn dance was held outside the old barn, which was itself subsequently transformed into the Harrow Museum and Heritage Centre.

In 2002 the restoration is still far from complete. When this picture was taken in the summer, the most vulnerable part of the main manor was literally under wraps until further work could be carried out.

The present site of Pinner Park Farm, seen here in the 1960s, has close links with Headstone Manor. Six centuries ago much of its land was enclosed for use as a deer park by the archbishops who then resided at the manor. Until relatively recently the present farmhouse, which dates from the mid-1750s, shared its yard with a large granary (left) which was built in about 1800.

Once it was no longer required for its original purpose, Pinner Park's granary could have fallen into disrepair. Instead the whole structure was lovingly moved to Headstone Manor, where it is now a popular visitors' attraction.

There is still a working farm at Pinner Park and the farmhouse remains. In 2002, however, it is no longer wholly the dairy farm that for most of the twentieth century was famous for producing, bottling and delivering its own milk.

Now the farm has been literally cut in two by the busy dual-carriageway, George V Avenue, much of Pinner Park remains as open space. Motorists, especially those who observe the 40mph speed limit, may still enjoy surprising views (for a London borough) of cows and other livestock.

Hatch End Farm in Headstone Lane had only 75 acres, but at its heart it could claim this beautiful sixteenth-century farmhouse. In the 1830s the land was bought by the London and Birmingham Railway Co. for its line through Pinner and Harrow, but parts were subsequently leased back for farming.

Opposite: In more recent times Letchford House has undergone further changes for use as offices. Its grounds now carry a Harrow Heritage Trust plaque identifying it as 'the probable home' of Dr John Letchford, who was buried in the chancel of Pinner Parish Church in 1666.

Over the years Hatch End Farm has changed not only its function but also its name. By the late 1960s it had become a private residence called Letchford House, a name it shares with the nearby Letchford Arms. Both farmhouse and pub were once owned by the same farmer, George Mold.

The prolific artist B.C. Dexter has left us this charming reminder of the Chantry, the long-since vanished house reputed to have marked the site of the original medieval chantry of 1324. Today the name is kept alive by Chantry Road and Chantry Place.

Opposite: From the 1930s onwards the Chantry area has been developed for light industry. Today the surviving cottages have an extensive industrial park as their neighbour, occupied by companies engaged in such twenty-first century activities as crash repair and frozen food distribution.

In the days before the 1913 opening of Headstone Lane station the area known as the Chantry felt like a separate hamlet. This peaceful picture featuring a prominent roadside stand-pipe and water trough comes from a postcard dated 1902.

The Letchford Inn, as it was called on its opening in 1868, was built by the Mold family, who had previously run the Alma beerhouse in Harrow Weald. In this undated (but probably 1920s) view, the pub had already changed its name to the Letchford Arms.

Though exterior changes were made in 1928 and again in the 1980s, the original Letchford Arms can still be recognised today. Apart from the adjoining Letchford Terrace, also built by the Mold family, its present surroundings all date from the twentieth century.

Since it was the speculative builder who did most to change the face of Pinner, Hatch End and Headstone during the twentieth century, it is perhaps appropriate that our final page should recall the start of the building boom in the 1920s. The setting is the junction of Pinner Road with what was soon to become a built-up Headstone Lane.

In 2002 'the finest labour-saving homes in the district' – as promised on the hoarding in the picture above – extend the length and breadth of Headstone Lane. Even when allowances are made for the passage of time, the present occupants may still be surprised to learn that the average house, when new, cost only £850.

Acknowledgements

Although I have known the area since childhood, I cannot claim to be a 'Pinner man', as such, and am therefore regarded by those actually in residence to be in some way demeaned if not actually deprived! On one of my frequent exploratory tours this year, I was even asked – and by an old Pinner friend at that – what I was doing in the village without a passport.

Against this background, I must be especially honest in recording how much I have been helped by the published researches of the many who have gone before me, from the collected writings of Edwin M. Ware (1955) to Alan Ball's *The Countryside Lies Sleeping* (1983) and Patricia C. Clarke's *Pinner* (1993). In particular, I must single out the inspiration I have found in the immensely readable articles by the late Jim Golland that have enlivened local newspaper and learned journal alike for many decades.

Given that he had once made an invaluable contribution to the Pinner section of the 'Harrow Before Your Time' Exhibition, I had hoped that he would bring his unique knowledge and eagle eye to the reading of this text – but it was not to be. Instead this role has again been generously performed by Bob Thomson, Harrow's local history archivist, who has also given permission for the use of a great many old Pinner pictures from the Harrow Local History Collection.

As in previous volumes, other old pictures have been drawn from the archives of the *Harrow Observer* and from my own steadily increasing collection. The contemporary pictures were taken by myself.